MASTERING THE BASIC'S

Mastering the Basic's

GARY HAYWOOD

INTRODUCTION

Life becomes easier the moment you understand the forces shaping it. Most people move on autopilot, reacting, spending, agreeing, and hoping things work out. This book shifts you out of survival mode and into strategy.

Mastering the Basic's gives you the essential skills every adult needs: how to think clearly, manage your currency with purpose, communicate with confidence, and understand the real cost of living.

The basics are the true foundation of independence. When you strengthen them, everything else becomes simpler, your decisions, your relationships, your finances, and your future. You'll learn how to pause before reacting, question before accepting, and research before deciding. You'll see how communication shapes your opportunities and how income, time, and responsibility form the backbone of adulthood.

This isn't about being perfect. It's about being prepared. It's about gaining clarity, control, and confidence in a world that constantly pulls you in every direction. By the end of this book, you'll have a sharper mindset, stronger habits, and a clearer path forward.

Let's begin.

Part I

T^{he}

Basic Skills

Critical Thinking
Research
InterPersonal Communication

Critical Thinking

is the foundation of mastering the basics. It is the habit of pausing before reacting, questioning what you see, hear, and believe.

In a world built on advertising, opinions, and emotional selling, critical thinking is your first line of defense. When you think critically, you stop living on autopilot. You begin to see patterns, how currency moves, who profits, and what truly adds value to your life.

Mastering the basics is about training your mind to notice, analyze, and act with purpose.

Critical thinking means slowing down before you accept something as true. It's about noticing assumptions, asking what evidence supports an idea, and recognizing when someone is trying to sell you emotion instead of fact. When it comes to your income/currency, this is your first defense.

R esearch

means taking the time to compare, verify, and understand. It's the process of asking a question, gathering information from reliable sources, comparing what you find, and forming a clear conclusion based on evidence.

Good research isn't guessing or repeating what others say. It requires curiosity, discipline, and the humility to admit when your first idea was wrong.

Know before you decide. In a world built on convenience and impulse, research separates the informed from the overwhelmed. Whether it's a job offer, a loan, or any relationship, the person who takes time to research always comes out ahead.

Every decision should be treated as an investment, of money, time, or energy. You don't need to be an expert; you just need to be curious. Ask questions, look deeper, and learn the real cost.

Research gives you the power to choose with clarity.

Interpersonal Communication

is the exchange of information, feelings, and meaning between two or more people. It is one of many ways, we connect.

When you speak, listen, watch someone's body language, or even share silence, you are communicating. Communication includes tone of voice, facial expressions, word choice, posture, pauses, and attention.

Strong interpersonal communication means understanding and being understood. It's more than speaking clearly, it's expressing yourself with confidence, listening with purpose, and knowing when silence says more than words.

Good communication builds trust that money can't buy. *How* you communicate determines *how* the world responds. When you learn to communicate with honesty and respect, people listen and more importantly, they believe you.

Every relationship, business deal, and opportunity depend on this clarity. Being able to explain yourself clearly and confidently is power.

The True Cost of Living

The Exchange Cycle: Time for Currency

B eing alive has a price. Not just in dollars, but in **effort, responsibility, and discipline**.

Society connects adulthood with independence. When you're responsible for your own housing, food, and survival, your decisions carry weight, and that weight forges maturity and strength.

When you live in someone else's home as an adult, a different dynamic forms. Adults with normal capabilities living at home equals weakness, immaturity and laziness.

Adults stand. Children are held.

You need to develop the foundational abilities that allow you to stand on your own two feet.

Income/currency represents more than the money you earn. It's the foundation of your financial ecosystem. Every dollar that enters your life reflects your time, effort, and skill exchanged for value.

Understanding currency begins with recognizing its role as a tool, not a guarantee. When managed wisely it can create many opportunities for growth.

Learning to direct your income with purpose is a daunting task at first. Too often, currency arrives only to disappear into bills, interest, and impulse spending. True management involves planning where your income goes before it even reaches your hands, budgeting effectively between wants and needs.

- Income should work for you, not just pass through you.

- Effective income management extends beyond your primary paycheck.

- When you view income as a dynamic resource instead of a static paycheck, you shift from survival to strategy.

- Your time is traded for currency. That currency fuels your living expenses.

- This cycle is the backbone of modern life. But you can change it.

Working or earning an income is vital to survival in the United States because the nation's economic system is built on the exchange of labor for money — and that money grants access to the essentials of life.

Everything has a price, whether you pay in money, time, or effort.

Beyond survival, consistent income represents autonomy and power. It gives individuals freedom of choice: where to live, what to buy, and how to spend their time. In short, income is not just about earning it's about maintaining control in an economy where every necessity carries a price tag.

Cost of living expenses are the ongoing, essential costs of daily life: rent, food, utilities, transportation, and taxes.

These are recurring expenses that reflect what it truly costs to exist in society.

EPILOGUE

Mastering the basics is more than a skill set, it's a shift in how you move, think, and decide. By now, you've seen that life isn't controlled by luck, talent, or background. It's shaped by the choices you make every single day. The small habits. The steady improvements. The willingness to look at your world with clear eyes and take responsibility for each step.

This book is the foundation. But foundations are meant to hold something bigger.

As you apply these principles, thinking critically, communicating with intention, managing your income with purpose, you'll start noticing the areas of your life that need strengthening

If you're ready to build momentum and lock in the discipline that fuels growth: **Self EMS: Implementing Perpetual Success** shows how consistency turns small actions into long-term transformation.

If you want to see how these principles play out in real life, through struggle, redemption, setbacks, and victory, **The Haywood Saga(**a memoir'**)** offers the unfiltered journey of a man refusing to be defined by circumstance and choosing strength over excuses.

And when you're ready to take control of your finances at the highest level, **The Power of No Debt** breaks down the real path to financial freedom, one decision, one dollar, one mindset shift at a time.

Together, these works form a larger mission: life mastery through knowledge, discipline, and self-direction.

Your next chapter isn't written yet, because you're the one who writes it. And now, you have the tools to do it with clarity, confidence, and purpose. Keep building. Keep standing. Keep choosing growth. This is just the beginning.